Your Personal Information Is At Risk

A Guide for Protecting Yourself

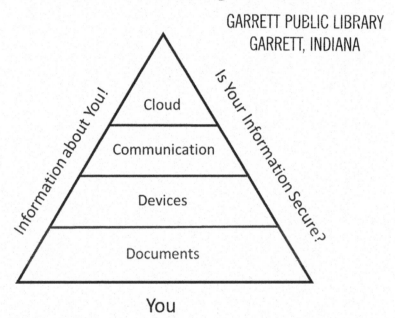

Information about You!

Is Your Information Secure?

Cloud

Communication

Devices

Documents

You

Another
Johnny Security Seed ™
Book By:

RICH OWEN

Your Personal Information Is At Risk

A Guide For Protecting Yourself

Rich Owen

ISBN (Print Edition): 978-1-09833-858-9

ISBN (eBook Edition): 978-1-09833-859-6

CONTENTS

DEDICATION

This book is dedicated to my grandchildren and to all
who have an interest in protecting their information.

PREFACE

This book began as just a small book for new users of smartphones. It was originally written for children and teenagers. It was soon realized that there are also older first time users of smartphones. There are many features that also spread into the world of the personal computer and accessing personal information online. The entire world of social media and email also needed to be explored. This led to security and privacy, and discussing how your data is stored or processed online.

Although this is all necessary because of the age in which we live, we have not totally gotten away from paper. Therefore this book is front-ended with steps that you should take to protect your paper-self as well as your virtual-self.

To my security brethren, you will note that I avoid getting too deep so as to avoid exposing the reader to areas where they could put them further at risk.

INTRODUCTION

We live in the Information Age. We are constantly asked to provide information about ourselves to verify our identity or value. To do so, we need to hold some elements of our identity to ourselves while other bits of information need to be publicly available. We need to be in control of the information that defines us. There are forces of evil that exist to collect as much information as they can about us. Granted, not all information collection is evil. Some information collection about us is "intended" to better serve us, but what happens when that well intended collection is exposed in a data breach? Some individuals and companies create profiles of data about us, defining our virtual identity. They can use that profile to influence our lives in a way that may not be in our best interests or worse, they may be able to virtually become us. Acting on our behalf, they can send email for us, access our bank accounts, and more. They can virtually destroy our personal, financial and emotional lives.

This book will examine several actions that you can take to physically protect your documents. For information about you that is in a digital form, we will explore ways in which you can reduce the risk that your data will be disclosed, modified, or just made unavailable even to you. The following diagram shows that we will create a foundation of protection based on our physical documents. On top of this, we will explore how your digital information is at risk and what you can do to reduce that risk in the devices that you use, the ways you communicate, and even data that you put, or allow to be put, into the cloud[1].

---

1   The term cloud is the collection of computers that are accessible via the internet, sometimes called the World Wide Web (www). When you access Facebook, your bank, a booking site on the internet you are accessing a computer in the cloud. That computer may be anywhere in the world.

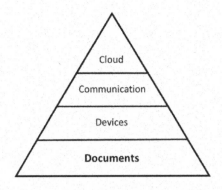

DOCUMENTS

We will begin by identifying what scraps of paper in your life may be of value. Then we will suggest steps to take to protect them.

Life

The following are examples of documents about you that you should consider protecting:

- Birth Certificate
- Social Security Number
- Driver's License
- Identification cards (student ID, etc.)
- Marriage Certificate
- Citizenship paperwork
- Divorce Decree
- Passport
- Last Will & Testament
- Death Certificate

- Living Will
- NDR
- Other

Education & Career

The following are examples of documents that you should consider protecting about your qualifications in life:

- High School Diploma or GED
- Other Diplomas
- Military Discharge paperwork (DD 214)
- College Degrees and Transcripts
- Profession Licenses and Certifications
- Medical records
- Other

Possessions

The following are examples of documents that you should consider protecting about the property that you own:

- Vehicle (car, truck, RV, etc.) Title
- Title to your home
- Title to other real estate that you own
- Other

Finances

The following are examples of documents that you should consider protecting about your ability to pay your bills:

- Bank Statements
- Vehicle Loans
- Real Estate Loans
- Stocks and Bonds
- Personal Loans
- Credit Card numbers and Statements
- Insurances (to protect against financial loss of person or property)
- 401k or IRA
- Other

Family

You should also help your family by providing them guidance in the protection of their information.

Protection of your documents

All of the paperwork about your life is not created equal and therefore it is not necessary to protect each document in the same way. That being said, let's examine the need to protect some of the above documents.

If you do not have your birth certificate or military discharge (DD 214) paperwork, you can get a copy sent to you, even though you may not need them right now. You may need your birth certificate to get or renew a driver's license. If you do not have a copy, this could delay your process. If you do not have a copy of your DD-214, showing prior military service, you may miss out on a veteran discount e.g. a new car, meal, etc.

The above are examples of preserving documents so that you have them when needed. Some other documents should be protected from the viewing of others. Examples of these are credit card numbers, Social Security Number, Driver's License numbers, and medical data.

Then there is the concept of utility of the information. You need to know your Social Security Number, but you should NOT carry your Social Security Card in your purse or wallet. If someone steals your purse or wallet and it contains you SSN, you have just made it easier for them to steal your identity. On the other hand, you need to keep your credit cards, driver's license and other identity information in your purse or wallet because you need it on a daily basis.

The best method of protecting these documents is a personal decision; it can range from a folder in a sock drawer, to a drawer in a file cabinet, to a safety deposit box in a bank. For about fifty dollars, you can purchase a lockable and fire retardant safe to store these documents. Obviously if you have other high value items, you will want to use a safety deposit box or safe.

Take a moment and review you physical world. Do you feel that you have done right for yourself?

Now we will explore how you can protect your virtual-self in this new digital world.

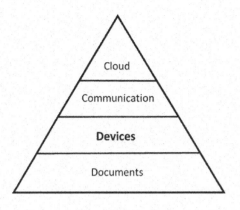

DEVICES

Your Virtual Self

The phrase "digital transformation" is in use by business today. It basically means to put as many processes and data into digital form and make them accessible online (via your phone or computer).

Protection of your information and data starts with you! No one will protect information about you, better than you. To that end, this book has been written to inform you of different ways in which information about you may be exposed and how to limit that exposure. This is not a book about how to use digital technology like smartphones and computers, or accessing data in the cloud. The focus here is to make you aware how you may be putting your virtual self at risk by the decisions that you make with your data. The objective here is to help you avoid becoming a victim of cybercrime.

If you go to the gun range to shoot a gun, there will be a safety officer with rules and guidelines on how to participate in activities on the range in a manner that will keep everyone safe. The range safety officer will not teach you how to shoot your gun. Modern computers are much like loaded weapons. If you are not careful, you can "shoot your eye out" (A quote from the movie "A Christmas Story"). Seriously, casual use of a computer can ruin your life emotionally and financially. To be forewarned is to be forearmed.

In today's world, it is no longer enough to be a good person and work hard for a living. Now, like a show dog, you need papers to prove your existence and value. No sooner are we paper trained, than we find there is an entire virtual replica of us in the digital world. Often times this virtual persona can drastically impact the real self. Just ask anyone who has had their identity stolen.

In the words of cyber security professionals, the objective of protecting your data is to ensure its **Confidentiality, Integrity** and **Availability**. Protecting the confidentiality of your data means that only you, and those people who you have authorized, may see your personal (including medical and financial) information. There are many state and federal laws that support this, but you need to know what **you** can do to protect yourself first and then hold others accountable. Ensuring the integrity of your data means that it correct and that only authorized people and processes may alter it. Availability of data simply means that your data is available when you need it. In some cases, this can only be assured by extra steps on your part, e.g. do you have a back-up of your data?

Privacy Points

- Privacy starts with you!
- There is an old saying that two people can keep a secret if one of them is deceased.

- Once you have given someone some of your information, you have lost control of what they do with it.

- Information that you put into the cloud (email, tweets, social media) stays there FOREVER!

- There are bad guys who are constantly trying every trick in the book to get your personal data or trying to trick you into doing something that may cause harm to you or others.

Common risks with our Digital Devices

We will cover some of the things that can put your data at risk. In this section we will look at how the data is stored or used on your device, e.g. when we talk about an application or a game, it is one that only runs on your device and is not interactive with other devices. In the communications section we will examine ways that your data may be exposed in transit. In the section on the cloud, we will discuss several ways in which your data is at risk when under the control of others.

Hackers, Viruses, and Worms, Oh My!

Oh yes, just like in "The Wizard of Oz" where "Lions, Tigers and Bears, Oh My" were the threat, with your data it is more like **Hackers, Viruses**, and **Worms**.

First of all, a hacker is a person who is trying to access your device or data. That person may be sitting in your office at work, the house next door, or in another country. Historically, the hacker has been a young male, but that may be changing as we see more activity from state sponsored attacks. The hacker has many tools to use. He may use sophisticated tools to find ways to break into your computer or a computer where your data is stored, or he may create a program to trick you into helping him get access to your data.

What is called a virus is basically software that is up to no good, often times called malware. A computer virus is like a biological virus, it must be delivered to the potential host by a sneeze or touching an infected person for a biological virus, or via email for a computer virus. The point here is that the virus is the transport mechanism that delivers the payload. The payload is the part that causes you harm. The payload can do things as silly as turn your screen upside down, monitor everything that you do on your computer, take total control of your computer so that it can be used to attack other computers, or just cause your computer to no longer function. In the early days, viruses were spread via floppy drives as people shared games with each other, pre-internet.

A worm is like a virus except that it has the ability to move from host (computer) to host. This is like a thief at night that goes around checking to see if all of the cars in the parking lot are locked. If one is not, then he executes his payload of stealing what is in the car or the car itself.

Volumes have been and continue to be written about hackers, viruses, and worms and all of the evil that they cause. The most important thing for you to realize is that the threat is real. I have had people tell me that there is nothing on their computer that a bad guy would want, which is why they are not more careful. Note above, that the hacker may be able to see all that you do on your computer, like your ID and password for your bank account. From there he can do anything with your money. The hacker may be able to take over control of your computer. If he controls your computer he can use it to attack other computers or just use it to store illegal porn. Just think of the problems if your computer was discovered to contain child porn. Eventually you may be able to explain to the police that you did not do it, but will your friends and family ever really believe that some hacker did it, not you?

Viruses, Worms and Hackers typically trick you into doing something stupid or they attack vulnerabilities in computers and network systems.

Vulnerabilities

When any computer program is written, it is created to do a specific job. The programmers are focused on making that happen. The marketing people are interested in getting the program released by a certain date. For example, if a programmer is writing a program to help you do your taxes, it would be of little use if the program was not available until after the tax filing deadline of April 15. This is called time to market. With the keen focus of the programmer to make something happen and having to do it in a rush to meet a deadline, we end up with programs that may have flaws or what we call vulnerabilities. Sometimes a hacker can exploit the vulnerability. This is the reason why just about everything relating to a computer requires software updates. How many times have you updated the operating system on your phone or computer? In many cases this update is to patch vulnerabilities that exist in the current program.

Vulnerabilities can also be created in the way we configure our devices and networks. If you have made a change to your home Wi-Fi to allow you access to play a game, you may have created a vulnerability that someone else may be able to exploit.

Vulnerabilities are opportunities for the bad guys. Some devices have operating systems that make them less susceptible to viruses, but they all have vulnerabilities that may be exploited by hackers.

Backups

Whether on your phone or on your computer, your data can be lost if there is a hardware or software failure. If you would be impacted by loss of data on your devices, then you should create a backup of that data. If you do not have any sensitive (personal, medical, or financial) data on your device and you trust your cloud storage provider, then use it. If you have taken the extra step, like encryption, to ensure that your data can be protected in the cloud, then use it. If you are uncertain, make a copy of your phone data to your computer and make a copy of your computer data to removable media and then secure that media. Flash drives that plug into your USB port, sometimes called thumb drives, are very inexpensive. They are great for storing your data, but then you need to secure them separately from your devices. Consider the same fireproof safe that you are using for your documents.

Phones

Our phones may look different, but all phones have the same basic features. What we will explore in this section is how to protect the phone and the information it contains.

The guys at the store should have performed most of the set up for you. They should have connected you to a service provider that will allow you to call other phones and allow you access to the internet.

They should have made sure that your phone would automatically be updated with new features. This is important because sometimes phones have problems and they need to be fixed. Remember the comment above about time-to-market issues and vulnerabilities. Ideally your phone should be configured to back-up its configuration and data to the cloud. This way, if something happens to your phone, you will still be able to restore your data on this phone or on a new phone. If your phone is not backed up to the cloud, then you need to ensure that your phone is backed up to a computer that you trust.

It is now up to you to take good care of your phone. Make sure that you keep it safe and its battery charged. You should plug your phone into a charger each night. WARNING: You need to be careful where you plug your phone in to get the battery recharged. For best results, and to ensure your privacy, you should use the USB to AC adapter. You can also plug your phone into the USB connector on your computer. Plugging the USB connector into a charging station, like at the airport or a bar, or another computer may charge your phone, but there could be an attempt to access everything on your phone. You can get a special adapter to use when at a strange place. This adapter allows you to charge your phone while ensuring that the charging station will not allow any access to your data.

Also in the area of proper care of your smartphone is the task of ensuring that you keep it current. In many cases it can do much to protect itself if you let it. You need to ensure that when the phone indicates that the OS (operating system) needs to be updated, that you do so as soon as possible. In some cases, this new version of the OS may provide new features, but in many cases the new version is there to fix a flaw or weakness that has been discovered in the current version. In many cases, once you have updated your OS, you may notice that some of the applications on your phone require an update. Typically there is a setting in your phone that will automatically update outdated versions of applications for you. Generally the phone is smart enough to only do this when you are on a free network.

Because of the operating system, some smartphones are more susceptible to viruses than others. We will discuss viruses in more detail in the section on computers. Depending upon your phone, you may also need some anti-virus software running on your phone.

Although more popular on computers, it appears that some phones are now being attacked by what is called ransomware. This attack comes via email where it tries to trick you into clicking a link to a bad website. You can also get ransomware by going to a bad advertisement on a good web site. When you click on the link, you may have allowed the bad guys to take over control of your phone. When they have control of your phone, they can do anything. In some cases they install ransomware. This is software that is loaded onto your phone that encrypts all of the data on your phone. This makes your phone unusable unless you pay the bad guys whatever they are demanding. This is a good time to have created a backup of your phone so that you can reset the phone to factory settings and then restore your system and data from backup.

The important thing is that this phone is yours. It is the right thing, in most cases, to share with other people, but not with your phone. You need to make sure that no one does anything on your phone that could break it. More importantly, you need to understand that anything done on your phone will appear to be done by you.

How does my phone know that it is me?

Your phone is a single-user device. This means it expects only one person to use it. To help you make sure that no one else uses your phone, it requires you to verify yourself as the owner. Some phones use face or fingerprint recognition. Most phones also require a password when the other recognition method fails. In most cases, this password is four to six numbers. This is called a PIN (Personal Identification Number). You should use numbers that you can remember, but that others would not guess. Your birthday or 123456 are examples of bad PINs.

It's a Smartphone.

Smartphones are like small computers. Each thing that it can do has a special button (they call an **Icon**). You push the icon and that function will make something happen. You can also add features or applications to your phone by going to the application store on the phone. This can be tricky. The new thing that you want may cost money to buy. It may be free, but it may cost some of your allocated bandwidth to download from the store. Some new features, games, and programs may also cost money to fully use. Then there are the really bad and sneaky programs that try to trick you into telling it things that you should not. Some applications that you can install on your phone have a EULA (End User License Agreement). Many of the EULA's are long and written in legal terms. This legal statement is to protect the company that created the application. The question that you must ask yourself, when confronted with a EULA, is why are they asking me to agree to something? Some EULA's will explain that if you accept the terms that you are giving that application full access to everything on your phone. This is certainly a case of "Buyer Beware!" We will discuss this again in the section on applications.

Some applications require you to use an ID and a password to access it. Password selection is very important. Password creation will be covered in more detail in the section on applications. The key point here is to NOT use the same password for games and social media as you do for critical applications that provide access to your financial or health information.

Personal Computers

To keep things simple, this section will cover all personal computing devices which includes personal computers, Apple products, notebooks and even game consoles. These are all multi-user devices. This means that all users must identify themselves to the device. Personal computers, using the Microsoft operating system, may be more vulnerable to viruses but all computers are susceptible to attack by hackers, especially if they are using social engineering techniques.

The first step in protecting your data is to protect the device that contains it. This means do not forget to physically protect your computer (notebook) if you decide to work remotely. Most people think of protecting their computer when it sits in front of them on a desk, but the computer you take with you has your data as well.

Keep your computer's operating system up to date! Do NOT click on notices on a web page or in an email to do an update. Only accept update notices from alerts in your system. Updates also apply to applications. A weakness in an application can be exploited to allow a hacker to also take over control of your computer.

Using anti-virus, anti-spyware, and anti-malware is a smart move for all computers although they may not be needed for game consoles. Personal computers are more susceptible to viruses. Scanning email for potentially bad attachments is important on all devices. Beware, only use known good anti-virus (end-point protection) programs. In the early days of anti-virus software (around 1986), there was a product called Flu Shot. Versions 1 & 2 were a good start, but the advertised Version 3 was a virus. There are several good end-point protection solutions to select from, some of which are free to the end user. If you do not have this software, you should do a search for anti-virus software and load one onto your computer now. The main advantage of software that you pay for typically is in the updates and support should you have a problem. Some software goes the extra step of opening the email and trying to execute each link before it gives the email to you. This is a good step if you can afford it, but still it should not replace you being very careful in reading each email that you receive.

Remember, it is your data on the computer. What would you do if your computer died? You should keep a backup of all data (including pictures) that you care about. It is recommended that if you have a cloud storage service, use it. We will discuss precautions about the cloud later. You should also have a USB (thumb) drive that you periodically back your data up to. By putting a copy of your data on a thumb drive, you can store that drive in your fire proof safe where you are storing your paper documents. The trick here is to store your data in a manner that makes sense to you and that you occasionally check to see if you can recover the data. Also, when you store your data in a manual fashion, sometimes you may forget to do a backup. Create yourself a calendar entry to remind you.

Complexity is the enemy of information protection.

How does the computer know that it is me?

Unlike a Smartphone, a computer is designed to be used by several different people. This allows the computer to be configured to your needs. Therefore, you need a way to let the computer know that you are the user. The first step in this process is to create an ID. To verify your identity to the computer, you will need a password or some other method to authenticate your ID.

On a smartphone your identity is verified via a PIN or possible biometrics, like face or finger print recognition. There are three major ways to authenticate your identity. You can provide to the computer something you know, like a password. You can authenticate your ID to the computer with something that the computer knows that you have. This is often a small fob on your keychain that shows you a different random number every minute. The computer knows the code that is running on that fob and therefore knows the code it is showing. The third way of verifying your identity is via something about you. Examples of this are fingerprints and facial recognition. In some cases you will use more than one method. For example, you may log onto a computer with an ID and password. The computer or program may send a special code to your phone, because you previously told it your phone number. This is called two factor authentication and is highly recommended when accessing computers or programs that contain your highly sensitive information like bank or health data.

For most access to computers and games, people still use passwords. The real question is, what is a good password? Your password should not be easy for someone to guess. If they do, they can use it to pretend to be you. If they do get into your computer or program, what harm can they do? Think about that for a second. Would you really want someone in your computer? They could not only see all of your data, the may be able to read your email, send email from your account, or access your bank or health records that are stored remotely.

Many of us have used passwords for years. The conventional wisdom is that passwords should be eight characters long and use a mix of numbers, special characters, and upper and lower characters. Regretfully, these special conditions are forced on the user by some systems. Even then, there are some bad guys that have tools that help them crack or guess weak passwords. The best password should, again, be something that you can remember and one that someone else could not easily guess. Ideally, passphrases of more than fifteen characters (even without numbers and special characters) are best. For example, you may have a password that is "TheQuickBrownFoxJumpedOverTheLazyDog'sBack" or "2Bo~2Btit?" which means "to be or not to be, that is the question." How good does your password need to be? That all depends on the system to which you are trying to authenticate your identity and what would be the impact to you if someone else was pretending to be you.

If you are using your computer for important stuff like work or school, or if you keep important information on your computer, then you may want to have a very good password. If you are just using your computer to play games and you don't care if someone else uses your computer, then a simple password will work.

The selection, protection, and use of your password is very important. Some computer internet browsers will store your password for you for each application. This is a good feature as the passwords are stored in your computer for your use and so that you do not forget them. This does not work as well for applications that you also access via a phone. For that, you may need to use an application that runs on both devices. There are several good programs that are available and free, like PassKey or Password Safe.

Using a computer away from home.

When using a computer at work or someplace else, you should always log out when you are not going to be in front of the screen. If you do not, then someone can come in behind you and do whatever they want on that computer and it will appear that you did it. This is especially important where the computer is open to the public like a kiosk or in a hotel business center. There you should NEVER enter any information more important than your boarding pass information.

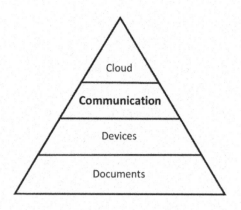

COMMUNICATION

As the previous section was about the device, this section will be focused on communications with that device. Mainly, we will be exploring phone calls, emails, and messages. Communications with the World Wide Web, with remote applications in the cloud will be addressed in the Cloud section of this book.

Phone

The telephone has been around since before most of us were born. We have all used the phone, so why a section on the secure use of your cell phone? Simply, the threat has changed. There is now a very active threat where people call you and try to trick you into giving up information that you should not. A good first step in protecting your phone is to know who is calling. Ideally, you should keep the names and numbers of friends and family in your contacts list on your phone. That way all you have to do is press the Phone Icon and their name to place a call. The added benefit of them being listed in your phone is that your phone will identify them to you when they call.

If you get a call from someone who is not in your contacts list, then you need to take a STRANGER DANGER approach to answering the call. This is very important. There are bad people in the world. Just because someone can call your number does NOT mean that they know you. When in doubt, do not answer the call. Let it go to voice-mail. Voicemail is like an answering machine. It will record messages for you when you do not answer your phone. If someone really needs to get in touch with you, they can leave a message and you can call them back. Another warning here, just because they leave a voicemail does not mean that they are not still trying to trick you. There are even ways for the bad guys to make a phone number appear to be from someone else, like the President of the United States, the Police, Hospital Emergency Room, etc. If the voicemail sounds important, you should show it to a person who you trust and get them to help you determine the right thing to do. You need to be very careful.

Let me repeat myself here. You will get calls, not only from people who you do not know, but the caller ID may say Wireless Caller, Unavailable or Unknown. Take that as a hint. If they do not want you to know who they are, then do you really want to deal with them? STRANGER DANGER!

Never give your personal information, like credit card numbers, to someone who calls you. If you need to give someone a credit card number over the phone, call them at a number that you know (separate from this call). After you have met someone, you can put their name and number into your phone so that you will know who it is the next time that they call.

Answering your phone is like letting someone into your home. Would you let a stranger in? Think about this for a minute. If a guy from the cable company shows up at your front door, he is usually wearing a uniform and has an ID. If you were not expecting him, you can call the cable company to verify who he is and why he is there. You should do the same with your phone. Look at the sections in this back of this book for checklists of what to do.

Phone Scams

The following are phone scams that have been received. The purpose of providing these examples are to make you aware of some of the horrible scams that are being used today. This is not the entire list. Following the description is some guidance as to what to do about each call. WARNING: These are scary, especially if you read them and think about what you would do if you got one of them.

1. Grandparents

The caller says that your grandchildren have been kidnapped and that if you do not pay immediately with a credit card you will never see them again. This is usually done when the caller has determined, via social media, that the grandchildren may be on a plane or otherwise unavailable for you to get in touch with them to verify that they are OK.

- If you simply ask the caller for proof that they are OK, the caller will typically just hang up.

2. Police – warrant for arrest

The caller says he is with the police department and that a warrant for your arrest is about to be issued because of an unpaid parking ticket. If you pay the fine immediately via credit card no warrant will be issued otherwise expect the police to be at your home in the next 24 hours.

- This is so bogus that there is even a video on the web of a Chief of Police receiving this call. She told them to come get her and gave them the address to the police station.

3. Social security

The caller says that he is from the Social Security Administration and they have discovered that they over paid you. If you do not refund the money to them immediately, via credit card payment, then your social security number and future payments will be suspended.

- This is just another scam aimed at senior citizens and others on a fixed income where the interruption of pay would be disastrous.

- I have received this call several times from Unavailable, Unknown, Wireless caller and from a local number. Remember the caller ID can be spoofed to appear to be whatever they want it to say.

- A variation to this call states that someone else has access to your social security and if you do not press "1" to address this problem that your social security payments will be cancelled. By pressing "1" you are making a call that is harder to trace and they will be asking you information about your identity. Just hang up!

4. IRS

The caller says that they are from the IRS and that you owe back taxes. You can correct this problem immediately with a credit card or the IRS will begin action to seize all of your property and bank accounts.

- This is most common around tax filing deadlines.
  This is very bogus. Besides, how did they get your cell phone number?

5. Computer Anti-virus

The caller may appear to come from a local number. The caller says that the virus protection on your computer has just been renewed.

Your credit card has been charged $360. If you have questions about this please call and they give a number.

- First of all they did not identify themselves. They did not even identify you. They just called your number. Their objective is to get you to call their number so that they can ask you questions about your credit card number to verify the transaction. They do not have your credit card number until you give it to them.

- A variation on this scam is that the caller says that the company that was providing security to your computer has gone out of business and that if you want a refund of money that you paid for that service please press "1" so that we can help you process that payment. This is like the previous version, a phishing exercise.

- In the either of the two examples above, they can ask you to inter a command on your computer to automatically refund the money owed to you. Here they are trying to take over control of your computer.

6. Lotto Scam

There is the lotto scam where they try and tell you that you won the lottery, remember the one that you never played. All that you have to do is give them your bank information so that they can put your money into the bank. NOT SO! They want to take money from your account. They may ask you to send a check of a couple of hundred dollars for legal fees and they will then send you a check for millions. NOT SO!

- This scam actually predated the common use of cell phones.

7. Unknown

I received a call from an "Unknown" caller. He introduced himself with a name and said that he was following up on a request that I made to buy insurance. Before I could say anything he said he just needed to verify some information. He asked if I still live in Arizona, which he could have guessed from my area code. I said yes but that I did not request any insurance. He just kept on talking to try and "verify" information. I told him that I did not request any insurance and hung up. He wanted to continue to ask me questions to get as much information out of me that they could. Most likely he only had the phone number. From the information that he would gather on this call he could create a better call or email for later use.

8. Unavailable

I received what sounded like an automated call from a major online retailer. The message was that they noticed some potential fraud on my account and that my card was being charged $1,247. If I did not make this purchase, then I should press one to be connected to an agent that would stop that transaction. Actually, if I had pressed one it would have been an opportunity like the previous example for them to extract as much information from me that they could, especially credit card data.

- This happens on retail accounts like Amazon or even banking accounts.
- Independently check your account.

General Rules for accepting a call on your Cell Phone

- If you do not know the caller and if you were not expecting a call, then let the call go to voicemail.
- Review the voicemail message and decide what to do.

- Reminder – STRANGER DANGER

You've Got Mail! (Email)

Before email, many companies used printed memos to exchange information. Then computers enabled messaging between computers and then messaging between users of the computers or network. Thus email was born. In many businesses today email is considered official correspondence. Access to your email account requires you to have an ID and to authenticate that ID with at least a password. Here again, I need to stress the importance of choosing and using a good password. You do not want to share this with anyone. You need to make sure that it is something that you know and it is not guessable, like your birthday. If someone gets into your email account they can send email to anyone and everyone from your account. They can embarrass you, take illegal actions on your account and trick others into being hacked as well.

By now, I expect that you know how to create email and get email, but the big issue here is learning how to READ the email. Now, I am not talking about teaching you a foreign language. You need to understand the parts of an email and how the bad guys can try and trick you, or lie to you. Many people get their email on their phone as well as on a computer. On the phone you can be more at risk, because you may not be able to see all of the details about the email.

The Basic Email

Your basic email has five or six main parts:

- Date & Time sent:
- From:

- To:

- Subject:

- Attachment: (may not be in every email)

- Text or body of the email message.

Mon 9/14/2020 12:03 PM

Rich

This is the subject field. This is first attempt to get your attention.

To

The body of the message is here. This is where you will be influenced to take some action: reply to the email or click on a link that will connect you to another computer.

Let's explore each part:

DATE/TIME:

- Although this is usually not significant, you should at least notice when the email was sent. If it was at a strange time, it may just be the bit of information that wants you not act on a bad email. Notice in the example above that this email was sent on Monday 9/14/2020 at 12:03 PM.

FROM:

- Ideally, this would show you the name of the person who sent the email. In the above example is shows that it is from Rich. I have removed the rest of the details of the sending email address. It is like a return address on a letter. You may recall that all letters that you get in the regular mail do not have a return address. Some letters that you get have a false or phony return address. This is the same with email.

- The biggest problem with the FROM field on the phone is that you only get to see what the sender wants you to see. On a computer, in some cases, you can see if the email was sent by someone else. You may see a FROM address of "Sally Jones," but it is really from fred@joesfishmarket. com (certainly not Sally). Look carefully as to where the email is coming from the data provided between the < >. You can generally see this level of detail on a computer, but often cannot see it on a phone or some email applications. In some cases, on a computer, you can actually examine the message header to see where it really came from. This is awkward and is generally only done to prove that the email is bad.

- The point here is that if it says that it is from Sally, it might be. It might be from someone who spells her email address like Sally but she is not really Sally. For example, let's say that you are expecting an email from Sally.J@gmail.com and you get an email from Salley.J@gmail.com or SallyJ@gmail. com would you catch the difference? Yes, go back and read the last sentence very carefully. As mentioned in the above bullet, this email might not be Sally who you thought it was. There is also the case that maybe someone guessed Sally's email password and are now sending out information from Sally's email account.

TO:

- You got the email, it must be addressed to you. Some email has the TO field blank (no name) or just says to Recipients. Both of these should be warning signs that you are about to be lied to or tricked. At least you should be aware that it is

NOT addressed to you specifically. In the above example I have reviewed the name of the recipient.

SUBJECT:

- This should be a clean short description of what the email is about. Sometimes this is just part of the lie that is coming your way. Typically this is something emotionally evoking to get you to open the email. Were you expecting an email with that subject from that person?

ATTACHMENT:

- In the above example there is no attachment. Every email does not have an attachment. The attachment could be an infected file. Many anti-virus programs catch this type of infection.

Generally pictures or PDF files are safe unless they have a link in them. There will be much more discussion about links later in this document. Unless you know the person and where this link is going to take you, "Do Not Click the Link". One trick with a PDF is for it to have a link in it for you to click on. Don't click the link.

If an attachment contains a word or Excel file, beware. Those file types have the ability to have programs imbedded into them. For example you may get an Excel spreadsheet that says that this file contains the names and address of people infected by a human virus in your area. All you need to do is to click the button in the file that says retrieve data or enable micros. If you do, it will allow a program to run that can access your system and do whatever it wants with your computer and your data. In short, this is bad.

BODY OF THE EMAIL:

- One would think that this would be simple, but with our continually improving technology, we take every possible step to complicate our lives for the purpose of making things easier and in return we make things more risky.

Let's explore how things could go wrong.

Questions to ask yourself when getting an email. Let's take something as simple as Sally sending you the following email:

- Date: Yesterday afternoon

- From: Sally

- To: It is not addressed to you by name, but the email showed up in your inbox

- Subject: Lunch

- Attachment: Menu.pdf

- Text or body of the email message. (as follows): Let's do lunch Thursday at 11:30 at Joe's Fish Market. This is the link to it so that you can determine how to get there. www. JoesFishMarket.com

What could possibly be wrong with the above?

1. Do you know Sally?

2. Is it the Sally who you think you know?

3. Since you cannot see the real address you do not know that it is from Sally. If you press reply what address will the reply go to? (don't send it – this is just to test the address)

4. If it is the Sally that you know, were you expecting a lunch invitation from her? Is this a normal correspondence

between the two or you?

5. The fact that your email address is not in the TO area is a warning. It is like the email was sent to many people, not just you. This is not normal.

6. Subject: There is no issue with the subject unless you never had lunch with Sally before.

7. Attachment: The attachment could be infected with a bad program. The problems here are more serious on computers, but it could still be an attachment that tricks you into providing information. For example: It could say "Here is the Menu" you have been invited to dine with us by Sally. Please press the link to confirm your reservation. When you do, it asks you for your credit card info to hold your reservation for ten dollars.

8. The body of the text could read much like the attachment above. The trick here is to get you to click on the link and for you to be tricked into providing your credit card data. But you say, it is only ten dollars. Ture, but with your credit card data they can now go shopping and spend much more.

The above is tricky. It may have been a valid invitation from Sally. You certainly should have called her before you replied or clicked on any link in the attachment or in the body of the text. Even if the email came from Sally's email account, that account could have been hacked and someone is now trying to hack you or steal data from you.

The bottom line here is that you CANNOT casually read your email anymore. You need to read and understand each line and determine if you believe it to be real.

Now let's explore what I like to call **Evil Email**.

Evil Email

Scams, phishing for information, and potential for system/account takeover are only some of the evil that can come from email. The bad guys will try every trick in the book to get you to click a link or provide your personal data, especially a credit card number. The following is a short list of some of the scams that are popular in email:

- Fake Invoice –
    - Email that says here is your invoice, click to pay
    - Email that says your account has already been charged – click to see invoice.
- Documents or photos that you were expecting. (You really were not expecting – so don't open the attachments.)
    - Sometimes the link to the documents is bad
    - Sometimes the link pulls up a PDF that has a link in it that goes to a bad site.
- Package Delivery
    - We failed to deliver your package – click here for delivery instructions
- Lotto
    - You won the lottery that you never entered – click to get winnings
- IRS – especially during tax season
- Inheritance
    - You have an inheritance from someone you don't know
        - Click link to execute the transaction

- Call a number where they will ask what bank account to deposit the money and they will withdraw all of your money

- Send processing fee of a couple of hundreds of dollars and they will send you your inheritance by return mail.

- Subpoena

  - You are being served a court order via email and you need to click the link to verify or pay the fine. Failure to do so will result in your arrest. (Not going to happen. This is not a legal way for you to get a subpoena.)

- Streaming Service (Netflix, etc.) – all to get you to click the link – This has become hot with so many people working from home during the pandemic.

  - Special offer

  - Reduced service

  - Account has been changed

- Any Major Event – Pandemic, Election, Shooting, anything that can get your emotions

  - Examples from the Pandemic

    - You are at risk

    - Need PPE – order here

    - Where is my check from the Government

    - Notice of Facility closure

    - Notice of infections

    - Notice that meetings have been rescheduled – click her to see changes

- Zoom meeting request – when you click the link it takes you to a bad website that could infect your computer.

- Reopening of business

- Elections

  - This is another example of trying to get an emotional response from you

  - Watch especially for clicking the Unsubscribe link

Evil Email Examples:

WARNING – DISCLAIMER

The following are actual examples of bad emails. Companies mentioned here are victims of someone pretending to be them to trick you into making a bad decision. The bad guys, in many cases, have actually copied material from that company's web page to make you believe that the email is really from that company. Read the following examples very carefully to learn how to avoid the tricks and traps of the bad guys. Email like the following examples are the number one attack vector used by bad guys. You have to assume that any email that you get that is too good or bad to be true, most likely is not true. The bad guy can create attacks like the following in hours and close them down before the authorities catch them. They only need to trick you once to ruin your day.

1. PayPal - Unusual Activity on your account
The following is an example of a bad email that appears to come from PayPal.

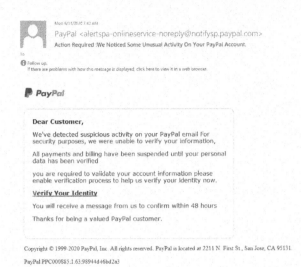

Mon 5/11/2020 7:42 AM

PayPal <alertspa-onlineservice-noreply@notifysp.paypal.com>

Action Required :We Noticed Some Unusual Activity On Your PayPal Account.

To

🚩 Follow up.
If there are problems with how this message is displayed, click here to view it in a web browser.

P PayPal

Dear Customer,

We've detected suspicious activity on your PayPal email For security purposes, we were unable to verify your information,

All payments and billing have been suspended until your personal data has been verified

you are required to validate your account information please enable verification process to help us verify your identity now.

<u>**Verify Your Identity**</u>

You will receive a message from us to confirm within 48 hours

Thanks for being a valued PayPal customer.

Copyright © 1999-2020 PayPal, Inc. All rights reserved. PayPal is located at 2211 N. First St., San Jose, CA 95131.

PayPal PPC000885;1.63;98944d46bd2a3

ANALYSIS:

FROM: This field appears to be convincing, but it just doesn't look right. It could have been created for this email attack or the sender may be masquerading as a valid PayPal email address. The message header of this email could have created this address so that it would look real. This alone does not give us information that we need to make a decision.

TO: This area is blank. This was not sent to me individually. {WARNING}

BODY:

Dear Customer,

We've detected suspicious activity on your PayPal email For security purposes, we were unable to verify your information,

All payments and billing have been suspended until your personal data has been verified

you are required to validate your account information please enable verificat https://vecwsi.com.au/heads/index.php y your identity now.
Click to follow link

Verify Your Identity

You will receive a message from us to confirm within 48 hours

In the body of the message it says Dear Customer. They are not even trying to act like they know who this is going to. Also notice the poor punctuation.

On your computer (you generally do not have this option on your phone), when you move your mouse cursor over the link in the email it shows an address of xxxxx.com.au/heads/index.php. The ".COM" is to fool you into thinking that this is a normal web site. Notice right after that there is an ".AU" which means that if you click on that link you will be talking to a computer in Australia.

ACTIONS THAT YOU SHOULD TAKE:

You can report this to www.IC3.org[2] in an attempt to allow the authorities to build a case and go after them. The most important thing to do here is realize that this is not real and it is an attempt to infect or take over control of your computer. Just delete the email.

2. Corona is not "controllable"

FROM: Says that it is from a SURVIVECORONAVIRUS.ORG (the actual address is long and confusing)

TO: *{Me by name}*

---

2   The web site www.IC3.org is a federal web site used by the FBI and Secret Service to collect data that helps them track down and convict people who send email like shown here.

SUBJECT: Corona is not "controllable"

BODY OF EMAIL:

CoronaVirus Pandemic Survival Guide

If you're one of those people who isn't concerned about the deadly coronavirus, you probably think they're coming out with a vaccine soon.

Well that's where you're wrong...

According to the Atlantic...

"Overall, if all pieces fell into place, Hatchett guesses it would be 12 to 18 months before an initial product could be deemed safe and effective."

12-18 months!

Millions can die in that time. Corona is spreading fast...

According to health.com: "coronavirus spreads faster than the flu" and it's now a "community virus" which spreads far faster.

Listen up.

The stupidest thing you can do right now is rely on your government/big pharma to protect you...

They worry about themselves before anyone else.

NEVER IN HISTORY has containment been done at such a large scale as is being done in Wuhan, China.

People are sealed shut in their homes..

Save yourself and family.

P.S. One sneeze on you is all it takes.

Survivecoronavirus.org

ANALYSIS:

FROM: xxxxxxx@SURVIVECORONAVIRUS.ORG (This is not a valid site. You can put this address into your computer browser and not only will it not show up as a valid web site. Also Google has articles of how this is a bad scam.)

TO: Yes, it was addressed to me. They could have gotten my email address from many places.

SUBJECT: It is the HOT Topic at this time. This in intended to make you worry and get you to click on the link.

BODY: You can read the body of the email. It is all aimed at getting you to click the link. The following is a small part of the real address and instructions if you were to click any of the above links:

https://xxxxx.xxxxxxx.net/ls/click?upn=KkJ-2FLYxwIpAXxp4Gt-GET-

It is unknown what would have happened if you had clicked the above link. In this case, the country code was the generic .NET, so you have no idea if it was real or not and where in the world that computer is. Once you click the link, they could have tried to trick you into giving up information on yourself or asked you for money. It could have also potentially caused your computer and some cell phones harm. This means that it could have made them unusable or simply taken over control and the bad guys could then just see all that you do and then masquerade as you to others.

Additional Warning. This message has an unsubscribe link. If you move the cursor of your mouse over that link you will see that you will go to the same place as if you clicked the other links. In other words, if you try to unsubscribe you may be asking for trouble.

ACTIONS THAT YOU SHOULD TAKE:

You can report this to www.IC3.org in an attempt to allow the authorities to build a case and go after them. The most important thing to do here is realize that this is not real and is an attempt to infect or take over control of your computer. Just delete the email.

3. Special Offer: SafeMask - BreatheEasy & Protected
The following are the details of the email. The actual email was very long with many pictures to make it look real.

FROM: Says that it is from a Safe Mask Offer (actual address is long and confusing>

TO: {Me}

SUBJECT: SafeMask - BreatheEasy & Protected

BODY OF EMAIL:

The body of the email had links and pictures to let you know that you could buy Safe Masks from them.

ANALYSIS:

When I moved my mouse cursor over the links and pictures in the email it showed me what address it would take me to. That address was very long and complicated and had nothing to do with the above company. This link pointed to a computer in Montenegro.

ACTIONS THAT YOU SHOULD TAKE:

You can report this to www.IC3.org in an attempt to allow the authorities to build a case and go after them. The most important thing to do here is realize that this is not real and is an attempt to infect or take over control of your computer. Just delete the email.

4. Anti-Virus is Out of Date

FROM: Says that it is from a known Anti-virus Partner <actual address is long and confusing>

TO: Me

SUBJECT: Activate your Anti-Virus Protection $date$!

BODY OF EMAIL:

ANALYSIS:

When I moved my mouse cursor over the above picture it showed me what address it would take me to. That address had nothing to do with the above company.

ACTIONS THAT YOU SHOULD TAKE:

You can report this to www.IC3.org in an attempt to allow the authorities to build a case and go after them. The most important thing to do here is realize that this is not real and is an attempt to infect or take over control of your computer. Just delete the email.

5. Anti-virus can expire
Just another example of the same as above, except now the sender is Internet Security.

ANALYSIS:

When I moved my mouse cursor over the above picture it showed me what address it would take me to. That address had nothing to do with the above company.

ACTIONS THAT YOU SHOULD TAKE:

You can report this to www.IC3.org in an attempt to allow the authorities to build a case and go after them. The most important thing to do here is realize that this is not real and an attempt to infect or take over control of your computer. Just delete the email.

6. Anti-Virus Protection May Expire $date$

Just another example like above except now this one is acting like it is from a different Anti-virus company.

ANALYSIS:

When I moved my mouse cursor over the above picture it showed me what address it would take me to. That address had nothing to do with the above company.

An additional threat here is that this email has an UNSUBSCRIBE Button at the bottom of the email. When you move your mouse cursor over that button it is the same address as if you were selecting the product. In other words, either way, you would allow the bad guys to take over control of your computer or at least infect it with a virus or ransomware.

ACTIONS THAT YOU SHOULD TAKE:

You can report this to www.IC3.org in an attempt to allow the authorities to build a case and go after them. The most important thing to do here is realize that this is not real and is an attempt to infect or take over control of your computer. Just delete the email.

The following are several examples of emails intended to trick you into thinking that you need to click the link to access your bank account. Many of these appear to be from Wells Fargo, but that is mainly because that is a big bank and you are more likely to have an account with them. Bank of America and other large banks are also targeted.

7. Alert Notification

ANALYSIS:

FROM: **Wells Fargo** Note that the address inside of the < > had nothing to do with the bank.

TO: Your email address. They do not know that you have an account at this bank. They just know your email address.

BODY: There may be several references and logos to the bank in the body. It is easy to get the logos from web pages and add them into an email.

Notice above that when you move your cursor over the link that it shows you the location of where the action will take place. In this case it was pointing to a computer in Vietnam (.vn).

In some cases, the bad guys will use links that look like they may be pointing to the bank. For example it may say WellsFargot.com (notice the t), Bank0fAmerica (notice the 0 instead of an "o").

ACTIONS THAT YOU SHOULD TAKE:

You can report this to www.IC3.org in an attempt to allow the authorities to build a case and go after them. The most important thing to do here is realize that this is not real and is an attempt to infect or take over control of your computer. Just delete the email.

OF COURSE, NEVER CLICK ON AN EMAIL FROM YOUR BANK. Go to the bank website that you normally use and do your business there!

8. Bank – Regarding your account

ANALYSIS:

FROM: *Name of a Bank* Note that the address inside of the < > had nothing to do with the bank.

TO: Your email address. They do not know that you have an account at this bank. They just know your email address.

BODY: Notice in this case they attempted to personalize it with my name. In this case they just repeated my email address. There are several references and logos to the bank in the body. It is easy to get the logos and add them into an email.

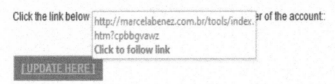

We recently determined that different computers have tried to log on to your account. . We now need more information to help us provide you with our secure service.

Click the link below [http://marcelabenez.com.br/tools/index.] er of the account:
htm?cpbbgvawz
Click to follow link

[UPDATE HERE]

When I moved my mouse over the [UPDATE HERE] button it was a very strange address. In this case it was pointing to a computer in Brazil (.com.br).

ACTIONS THAT YOU SHOULD TAKE:

You can report this to www.IC3.org in an attempt to allow the authorities to build a case and go after them. The most important thing to do here is realize that this is not real and is an attempt to infect or take over control of your computer. Just delete the email.

OF COURSE, NEVER CLICK ON AN EMAIL FROM YOUR BANK. Go to the bank website that you normally use and do your business there!

9. Just a strange notice that appears to come from the bank

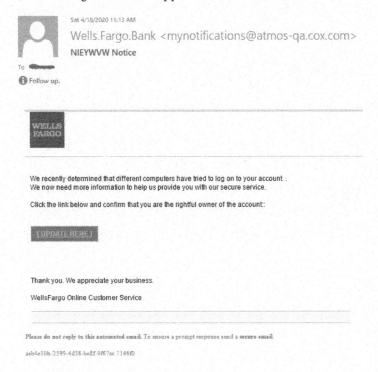

ANALYSIS:

FROM: What appears to be Wells Fargo, but actually is from a COX email account. On some computers you can examine the message header and it show you how that address was programed to appear on the message envelope.

TO: Me

SUBJECT: Very strange subject. It makes no sense

BODY: They want me to click the link to validate that it is my account. If I do, I will be giving them all that they need to go to the real bank and manage (withdraw) my money in my real account.

We recently determined that different computers have tried to log on to your account. .
We now need more information to help us provide you with our secure service.

Click the link b | http://dradanielacunha.com.br/beta/ | tful owner of the account:
index.htm?m7vqgfv4
Click to follow link

[UPDATE HERE]

Notice above that if you move your mouse over the link that says [UPDATE HERE] the computer will show you the address of the computer you will go to if you click that link. In the beginning string of characters above, note the last letters after the last "." before any "/". This is the country code. In this case it is a BR which is Brazil. You can use google to check country codes yourself to see where the link will take you.

Extra notice: They do not want you to reply because that may tip off the person who owns that account that his email account has been compromised. Also, this is an opportunity for them to suggest a secure email to them, trying to get you think they have your best interests in mind.

ACTIONS THAT YOU SHOULD TAKE:

You can report this to www.IC3.org in an attempt to allow the authorities to build a case and go after them. The most important thing to do here is realize that this is not real and is an attempt to infect or take over control of your computer. Just delete the email.

OF COURSE, NEVER CLICK ON AN EMAIL FROM YOUR BANK. Go to the bank website that you normally use and do your business there!

10. Coupons from businesses – An example here that appears to be from Costco.

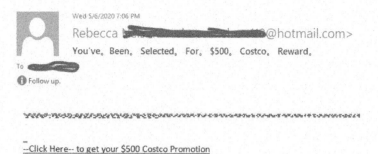

ANALYSIS:

Date/Time: 7 PM at night

FROM: Someone named Rebecca on a Hotmail email account. Why would someone named Rebecca be sending me a five hundred dollar gift card for Costco from a Hotmail account?

TO: me (we have determined that is easy to do)

SUBJECT: You have been selected for a five hundred dollar gift card

Although we all like free money the question of WHY is important here. What is in it for them?

BODY: Mainly the text is to get you to click the link. The link under CLICK HERE TO GET STARTED shows that you will be going to a computer in the cloud. Most likely it was just created for this purpose and will last just long enough to get you to go there and not enough time for law enforcement to find it. Who knows what would happen then?

ACTIONS THAT YOU SHOULD TAKE:

You can report this to www.IC3.org in an attempt to allow the authorities to build a case and go after them. The most important thing to do here is realize that this is not real and is an attempt to infect or take over control of your computer. Just delete the email.

OF COURSE, NEVER CLICK ON AN EMAIL FROM YOUR BANK. Go to the bank website that you normally use and do your business there!

11. Personal Extortion
FROM: Person that I do not know *

TO: Me

SUBJECT: *{a password that I have used in the past}*

BODY OF EMAIL:

I'm aware, *{a password that I have used in the past}*, is your password.

I need your full attention for the up coming Twenty-four hrs, or I will make sure you that you live out of shame for the rest of your existence.

Hey, you do not know me. But I know nearly anything concerning you.
Your present facebook contact list, phone contacts as well as all
the digital activity in your computer from past 168 days.

And this includes, your self pleasure video footage, which brings
me to the primary reason why I am crafting this e-mail to you.

Well the previous time you visited the porn webpages, my spyware
was activated inside your pc which ended up documenting a lovely
footage of your self pleasure play simply by activating your web
camera.

(you got a unquestionably odd preference btw haha)

I have got the whole recording. Just in case you think I'm playing
around, just reply proof and I will be forwarding the particular
recording randomly to 9 people you recognize.

It may end up being your friends, coworkers, boss, mother and
father (I'm not sure! My software will randomly select the contact
details).

Would you be capable to look into anyone's eyes again after it? I
doubt it...

Nonetheless, doesn't necessarily have to be that route.

I'm going to make you a 1 time, no negotiable offer.

Purchase USD 5000 in bitcoin and send them to the listed below
address:

1NPF*2baYztHU1q8kmWtYzjvYxa29ZWyfZG

[case-SENSITIVE, copy & paste it, and remove * from it]

(If you don't understand how, google how to purchase bitcoin. Do
not waste my precious time)

If you send this 'donation' (we will call this that?). Right after that, I will go away for good and under no circumstances make

contact with you again. I will erase everything I've got

concerning you. You may very well keep on living your current

ordinary day to day lifestyle with absolutely no concern.

You have got 24 hours to do so. Your time starts off as quickly you

go through this mail. I have an unique program code that will

alert me once you read this email therefore don't attempt to play

smart.

ANALYSIS:

FROM: This is an email from someone who I do not know. I suspect that this email address has been hacked and the owner of this account does not know that his account is being used to send messages like this.

TO: It is addressed to me

SUBJECT: The subject is a password that I have used in the past on accounts that I am not concerned about. It is not a password that I have used on any social media or especially work or banking account.

BODY: The body of the message is very explicit. My apologies, but this just goes to show how evil some people are. The threats in the email are all bogus because I have never used that password anywhere that I have any concern. Also, they cannot take over control of my computer (in this case) the way that they are pretending to do. I do not have a web camera on this computer. It is disturbing to see a password that you have used before in print in an email. You should read the email very carefully.

ACTIONS THAT YOU SHOULD TAKE:

You can report this to www.IC3.org in an attempt to allow the authorities to build a case and go after them. The most important thing to do here is realize that there are sick people in the world and just delete the email.

OF COURSE, if you have used that password on any accounts that you care about you should log onto that account and change the password immediately.

12. Some examples are just too obvious:

The link in the above email does not pretend to go to anything related to Apple.

13. Do you want/need a job?

Fri 7/17/2020 9:44 PM

David Taylor <Line2██████████pizza.com>

Looking for talent, I have found you-3I8HID-#-CB

To   David Taylor

🚩 Follow up.

J-STAR Co., Ltd.   Hiring

We are teaming with a nationwide, diversified financial services company to help them search for TR to join their expanding team

Our client continually tops Fortune 50's list of most successful companies and is looking for employees who want to grow professionally and personally within a company as well. We are looking to find motivated individuals who want to take part in a company's goal to move forward in global innovation in banking and financial services to join our growing team.

Responsibilities include:
Taking payments from customers
Answer questions about account
Data enter account information
Provide excellent customer service

Requirements:
Great communication skills
High attention to detail and accuracy
Ability to multitask
Great entry level opportunity

ANALYSIS:

FROM: This is an email from someone who I do not know.

TO: It is addressed to the person who sent the email. How strange is that?

SUBJECT: Looking for talent. We have a job for you.

BODY: The body of the message is very strange and general. The purpose here is to get you to reply to the email.

Several different things could be going on here. They could convince you that they have the job of the lifetime for you. They may direct you to a "what they call a SECURE site, https://" to enter your personal information to get the job. Their purpose is to collect as much data on you as they can.

In another case, they may actually work with you over the phone to get you to become a "Shipping Agent". They will explain that items will be mailed to you and that they will pay you to mail those packages to a different address. For this, they will put your salary directly into the bank. This is called a Mule. When people use stolen credit cards and they buy things online, they need a place to send the stolen times. That is you, receiving stolen items. This is a good cover for them because you are taking the risk and if discovered they already have access to your account, they can just remove any money that is left there.

ACTIONS THAT YOU SHOULD TAKE:

You can report this to www.IC3.org in an attempt to allow the authorities to build a case and go after them. The most important thing to do here is realize that there are sick people in the world and just delete the email.

Final Thoughts on email

If you believe that the email is bad or of no value to you, delete it. Some email clients allow you to mark the email as Junk Mail. This way, future email from that source will not end up in your inbox.

Guidelines for Email

- Are you sure this is from someone who you know?
- Were you expecting an email from this person?
- Does the subject and body of the email make sense coming from this person?
- Even if you know the person, if it contains a link – WARNING
- Reminder – STRANGER DANGER

Messages

In this section we will cover security issues that relate to messages. This is intended to cover all types of messages, tweets, Snapchat, Instagram, etc.

Just like phone calls, people who you do NOT know can also send you messages. If you get a message from someone you don't know, then STRANGER DANGER applies again. Delete it, no matter who it is from or what it says.

Also, when sending messages, be kind. People cannot tell if you are just joking or being serious when you write things that aren't very nice. Think about what you are writing in your messages and how the other person may read them differently than what you meant to say. I remember once telling someone that it was "No Problem." I meant that I can fix this and make it OK. The person got upset with me because to him it was a problem, and he could not believe that I did not see it as a problem.

The following are some examples of short cuts that are used in messages:

BRB - Be Right Back

BTW - By The Way

BFF - Best Friends Forever

CYA - Cover Your Ass

FOMO – Fear of Missing out

FUD - Fear, Uncertainty, and Disinformation/Doubt

GR8 - Great

ILY - I Love You

IRL - In Real Life

J/K - Just Kidding

LMAO - Laughing My Ass Off

LOL - Laughing Out Loud

NP - No Problem

OMG - Oh My God

RT - Real Time

THX or TX or THKS - Thanks

TMI - Too Much Information

TTYL - Talk To You Later

TYVM - Thank You Very Much

XOXO - Hugs and Kisses

Messaging applications, like most applications, require you to enter your ID and your password. Here again, this shows how important proper password use is. If someone can guess your password, then he can log onto your messaging application and send messages that look like they come from you. This recently happened to many famous people.

Message SCAMS:

Some messages have messages in them that are underlined. If you get a message that is underlined, the sender is trying to get you to go somewhere on the World Wide Web (internet). Unless you got this from a known friend, DO NOT CLICK ON THE LINK! – They are trying to harm you or trick you into giving up personal information about yourself. Just delete the message.

Guidelines for Messages

- If you do not recognize the sender – WARNING – Do not reply.

- If the message is not something that you were expecting, especially if it contains a link – DELETE IT!

- Reminder - STRANGER DANGER

Blended threats

A blended threat is one that uses a combination of different media and attack vectors. The following is an example of a call that I got from someone that said that they were from Microsoft Support. They told me that my computer was attacking the internet. The caller had no idea if I even owned a computer. They asked me to type some commands into the computer. The results looked like errors or something was going wrong in my computer. (This is an area where errors are normally logged. What I was seeing was normal). They said that those errors show that my computer was attacking the internet. They then told me that they would have to report that activity to the FBI, but since they were Microsoft support they could fix that for me. They tried to explain how they are the good guys, just here to help me. They didn't want money, but if I would just enter one command, they would be able to solve the problem for me. The command that they gave to me to enter, would have allowed them to take over total control of my computer. They would have been able to see all of my data. They would be able to monitor everything that I do in the future, including keystrokes. This would allow them to see my password for all systems that I log onto, including my bank. They would have been able to send bad and infected email from my email account. In the end they could encrypt my entire computer making it useless to me unless I paid them bitcoin.

Buyer Beware! "There's a sucker born every minute" is the phrase of con-artists. On the receiving end of phone calls, email, and messages, it is up to you to determine if the person is who they say that they are and is there a valid reason for you to accept the message. Even if you do, you need to be prepared to validate the source and the content of the message BEFORE taking any action.

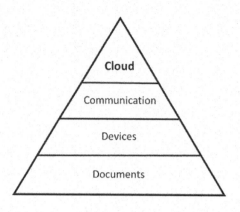

CLOUD

Your virtual world is the collection of data about you. This is data about you that is in your computer and in computers across the world, yes across the world. What is referred to as the Cloud is a collection of computers on the internet that you may or may not have access to. We discussed earlier the need for you to back up your data. We discussed putting a copy of your data on a thumb drive. If you have an account on a computer that is connected to the internet then you can simply save a copy of your data in that computer. The big difference is that you do not own or control that computer that is in the cloud. You are trusting that they will take care of your data and not share it with others.

You may be thinking that you never accessed a computer in another country and certainly you have never given your data to someone that you don't trust. In today's world that is just not so. In many cases when you access a site on the World Wide Web you have no idea where that computer is or how well the data is protected on it. Then you add the cases of data breaches that we have every year and it is hard to imagine your data not being in places that you do not approve. Your data is everywhere and most concerning in many places that you do not want it.

This section of the book will focus on your data external to your devices.

Internet (World Wide Web)

In the beginning viruses were delivered via floppy drives of people sharing games, but the internet has now made things so much easier. That is not to say that viruses are no longer on floppies, CD's or Thumb Drives, because they are. Most attacks are now automated and use email or a direct attack across the internet. If your computer is connected to the internet, then you are at risk of being attacked.

Browsers are special applications that allow you to access the World Wide Web. Every time that you go to a website with your phone or computer, it is like going into someone else's house. You do not know what to expect. You need to understand that you (your data) may not be safe. It is up to you to take the needed steps to reduce the risk of your data being exposed. There are some especially bad places on the internet where your computer can be taken over simply by you going to that address.

First, let's look at the browser. You use a browser to get information from the internet you will be providing that browser with information. Consider the following example. Let's say that you want to go on a vacation to the Grand Canyon. You use your browser to search for the Grand Canyon. You get what information that you wanted yet hours, days and even weeks later you continue to get extra notices on your browser from companies offering you services relating to you visiting the Grand Canyon. Why is that so? Have you ever read the privacy notice associated with the browser or application that you were using? Most of us have not. In many cases it is very long and full of legal words, e.g. not easy to understand. You can access this information in the settings area of the browser. As an example, a very popular browser has a sixteen page privacy statement that says how they will collect everything that you do and share it with marketing partners of course to better prove you with a quality service. Those sixteen pages are also full of links to other documents, so who knows how long the privacy statement really is. That same browser is tied to other internet tools which gather analytics on your usage, here again to provide you better service. They collect GPS & Wi-Fi data and data on applications that you access. Is this a problem for you? Let's say that the doctor just notified you that you may have a deadly disease. You are not sure yet, but you want to research it so that you can be prepared and so that you will be able to explain to your family. Someone else in your family may use your computer while you are logged on. Should they use your browser to search for something, they may see all of those ads for symptoms and how to deal with that disease. They now know that you have a problem. Is that an issue for you? Your privacy has just been violated. Some browsers have modes that do not collect that data. Some browsers let you control what is collected and shared. It is all up to you to know how you can control your data.

When you use a browser, the standard web page address starts with http:// {and the address of where you need to go}. When you enter that address into your browser it just provides a connection to that site. If you go to a web site that starts with httpS:// {and the address} then your connection to that site is encrypted. Sometimes your browser may show a little lock next to the address. This does not necessarily mean that this site is safe. It still could be a bad site. The "s" or lock just means that your communication with that site will be encrypted (secure from other people being able to see what you say).

There are even good sites that have advertising on them that may lead you to a bad site. If you do not know if the site or company is good, copy the name of the product and do your own research using Google, Bing or other search engine. Do not click on an advertisement or a link. With email you have already been exposed to how dangerous it is to click a link or go to a bad website.

When you do a search on the internet, often times the first items that come up in response to your query are advertisements. Some internet browsers even label these links with [AD]. This does not mean that they do not have the answer that you are searching for. This just means that they may want to find a way to sell you something.

So what can happen if you go to a bad site? Several things. First, you can be fooled into giving up personal information that you should not. Second, you could be fooled into sending money. If you give someone your phone number, they might share it with many more people and you may end up getting many useless calls. Third, the bad guys can just take over total control of your computer.

If you go to a web page and they want information, "YOU DO NOT HAVE TO TELL THEM THE TRUTH!" You do not know them! Think about any information that you give out. You can make up a phony identity for each site that you go to. The trick is in remembering, if you go back to that site, what information you gave to them. Once you have given out information about yourself to a stranger, you cannot prevent that stranger from sharing that information with others.

Firewalls

Most computers, especially those that use anti-virus or end point protection software have a firewall in them. The term firewall comes from the automotive industry. It is the safeguard that is put in place to protect the driver from the engine that creates power to the car through controlled explosions. A computer firewall is intended to allow you to access the internet while limiting the threats that it can pose to you. If you are at home or work, most likely you also have a modem that has an additional firewall in it. At home, an issue can come up when you install a device or game that needs extra ports opened for the device or game to work. Those extra ports may expose you to potential attack from the internet. In configuring these devices and games you need to be very careful.

Wi-Fi

Wi-Fi means a wireless connection that your phone or computer makes to the internet. If you are at home and your computer or phone is accessing the internet via one of your Wi-Fi devices over a secure connection then generally you are OK, unless you have made some changes to your home network, as mentioned in the firewall discussion above. If you are out shopping or at a place that provides free Wi-Fi then you are more at risk. Other people may be able to see and gain access to your computer and certainly you should never access important accounts (bank, medical, etc.) from this untrusted connection (without extra controls).

VPN (Virtual Private Network)

The VPN is intended to be like connecting a wire directly from your computer to the computer that you are trying to communicate with. This is a one-to-one connection that is encrypted so if someone was to see your data on the internet that they would not be able to understand what you are saying because it is encrypted. This is an excellent solution to use especially when accessing the internet from a Wi-Fi hot spot.

Guidelines for the Internet

- You should only go places on the internet that you know are good.

- You should not click on links from messages or emails.

- You should careful and think before you click on advertisements.

- It is a great source of information and danger.

Applications (Apps)

Applications are programs that run on your phone or computer. They were created for a specific purpose. You are familiar with many of them: the Phone app, the browser, the game app, the health monitoring app, the banking app, the conference app, etc. They all have a couple of things in common.

First, all applications were created to meet a marketing need and were created with a deadline. As mentioned in the vulnerabilities section, this means that they are naturally created with opportunities for the bad guy to exploit. Whenever you get an opportunity, you should ensure that all of your applications on all of your devices are running the most up-to-date version.

Second, for applications to work, they ask you for data, especially personal data. As with the discussion on the browser, you should know what they plan to do with the data that you give to them. The following are some screen shots from the EULA of a game application that could be on your phone.

- The type of your device, IP address, your game ID when using the app, and the country or region that you're playing in;

- Details about your gameplay on our app, including: amount of time played, if you have left the game on a specific level or if you have cleared it, and your scores on levels, and items you own or use;

- Purchase history on behalf of our payment service providers to keep a record on if a purchase has been successfully made. We do not collect credit card information;

- Information we collect via cookies and other similar technologies, as explained further below;

- Communications between you and us, whether in-game, via email, or through social media channels. We keep a record of these communications to provide customer service by answering your questions and providing you with a better experience using our app;

- Information from our other group companies or other third party companies who have your consent or have other legal rights to share granted information with us (advertising networks and publishing partners, platforms). This may include your interests, other games you played, demographic and general location information. We use this information as described in this Privacy Policy;
- Information that you provide when you connect to your social network account when creating an account with us. This may include, but is not limited to: your name, address, email address, or other information;
- information as further set out in this Privacy Policy, including Social sharing features , Marketing and Advertising

Notice that even this privacy statement has links to other notices.

Social Media

There are applications that allow you to share information with your friends and family. Some of the most popular social media sites are: Facebook, Twitter, LinkedIn, Instagram, Snapchat, Pinterest, Reddit and TikTok. You should make sure that you only share information on these sites with people you know, like family and very close friends. Even so, if you put some information into one of these sites, someone else can then share it with anyone else. Once something goes onto the internet, it is there FOREVER! You need to be careful to never say anything that you will be ashamed of in the future. At the time that this is being written, TikTok has come under a lot of questions by the security community. Some organizations, like the military, have banned its use. It is currently owned by China. The government is taking steps to band its use in the US. With this information you may want to consider how important that application is to your life. The same applies to all organizations that provide you a service for FREE. What is in it for them? What will they do with all of the data that they collect on you?

Some of these programs gather information about you—like where you are, where you have been, where you are going or what things that you like. If the bad guys have access and learn enough about you then they have a better chance of tricking you in the future. Reference the comments about privacy above.

Many of these social media sites come with advertisements and games. Here again, be very careful. You should ask, "When I play this game what are they getting from me?"

Sometimes you will be asked for personal information. This is especially true with a political donation. Often political donations require information about the donor. There may be a law requiring that information, but that information is now public. Maybe it is not such a big deal to share your name, address, phone number, birthdate, pay bracket, etc. but you should know that there are people who will use that data, especially with other data to create a profile on you. This will help the bad guys better trick you into giving up more information of value.

Likes & Comments

Be careful what you share about yourself. Comments that you post can be used against you. This also applies to "Likes." People can take your comments out of context and misrepresent what you mean. Other people may take offense to what you have said and search the internet for all they can find about you and post that information. Maybe it was not a big deal to share your email address or phone number when you did it, but now in the hands of people that disagree with you they may bombard you with calls and emails, or worst try to impersonate you.

Guidelines for Social Media

- You should make sure that your privacy settings only allow access from your friends.

- Do NOT share personal information with people that you do NOT know.

- Advertisements can be tricks.

Smile

Your phone and some computers can take pictures and even videos. The camera adds to your responsibility of being the owner of a phone or computer. You need to make sure that you do not take pictures of people, places and things that you should not. The best rule is "Would I want someone to take a picture of me doing that?"

Your phone will store your pictures. You can send copies to friends, but you need to be careful to whom you share a picture. Once you send someone your picture, you no longer have control of where that picture goes. Your picture can also let the person that you share it with know where you are. If you do not want your location to be known, then do not share the picture. Pictures and your locations are just some of the data that bad guys like to collect on you. They can use this against you later to trick you into taking actions that normally you would not do.

Financial, Medical and other Sensitive Applications

If an application uses sensitive data on your phone or computer, then you need to take special care about the privacy of that data. First, you need to carefully review the comments about passwords—how to create, not reuse, and do not share. You need to pay special attention to the EULA or any other agreement that you have wit that company. You need to understand that your data is now available via the cloud, by you and potentially others.

Credit Monitoring

There are companies that will monitor your financial records and alert you if someone has tried to access them to open a loan or do other financial actions. This is recommended especially if you access your data remotely, via phone or computer.

"Do you want to play a game?"

The games that we will discuss here are multi-player games. For these games, you need to create a logon ID and then a password. DO NOT use the same password that you use anywhere else. If you use the same password as you do for your bank then if this game gets hacked then the bad guys have your password and just need to figure out your ID.

DO NOT share personal information about yourself. The more the bad guys can learn about you, the better they are at creating a profile on you. A profile allows them to create emails or messages that will trick you into making mistakes.

Not all games and applications are good. Some are there just to gather information about you, from you, from your phone of who you talk to, where you have been, and what you buy. Some applications ask if they can track your location so they can send you information specific to your area. This also allows them to know and let others know where you are. Some applications will push notifications to you. The location and push of notifications you can control in the settings section on your phone. You need to think about what others know about you. When playing a game with someone on your phone or computer, you should never tell them your real name or anything about you. You need to think about what others know about you.

Guidelines for Playing Games

- Know if it will cost to play or continue to play.

- If a multi-player game, do not share personal information with other players.

- Know it is a great source of entertainment but there is danger that other players can gain information about you to be used against you later.

Data Storage

As mentioned previously, it is important that you back up your data. The cloud can be a great place to store a copy of your data. The trick is in how you get your data out. If you want to remove it can you be assured that it is gone? What controls are in place to protect your data? If you decide to store sensitive (financial or medical) data in the cloud you should use some form or encryption.

SUMMARY

Lies

I was fortunate. My seventh grade teacher taught me how to read the newspaper. No, I was taught to read earlier. My teacher taught me to read and understand what the point of view was of the person who wrote the article. In other words, how they are likely to twist the facts or avoid the facts. This has nothing to do with you protecting your information online. You need to understand that in the virtual world, the person on the other end your communication, in most cases, does not know you and has no issues with lying to you. This book is being written during the last several days leading up to the Presidential election. There are way too many examples of lies to list here.

Misuse & Fraud

Misuse of data is often what happens when you respond to email or to advertisements on the internet. Companies will gather your data and then share it with others, without your permission. This is just a reminder that with the internet, you are connected to the world. Everyone in the world is not nice. In fact, activity by some nation states to collect and steal data has increased over one hundred percent in just the past five years.

Risk and Risk Reduction

You cannot totally protect your data. All you can do is reduce the risk that your data and systems will be used as you have defined and with minimal risk of data or system loss. Risk is defined as the likelihood and impact of a threat acting upon a vulnerability. Above, we discussed some threats. We also discussed some vulnerabilities. You still need to access your data yourself and at times move it to trusted places. For example, you need to access your bank records. To do so, you need an ID and a password. If you have the right combination, you get it. If a hacker has your ID and password they get in and can act as you. The vulnerability of access is matched to the threat of a hacker knowing your ID and password. If your bank uses an extra level of authentication, where they send a code to your phone, then you have reduced the risk of the hacker successfully accessing your bank records. There is not one control that reduces all risks. The best approach is to use a layered approach of several controls to reduce the risk. That way, if one layer fails you still have a chance of not having an exposure of your data. As a last line of defense it is good to have credit monitoring or insurance to cover losses that you may experience if your data is compromised. You need to be a good filter for who you trust.

Bullies

Just because they are not in front of you and would knock you on your ass if you said something wrong to them in person is no reason that you should think you can be rude to people online. Remember, even with emoji's, it is really hard to tell exactly what someone was meaning when he sent a message. Send kindly, and receive with grace. We just need to be nice to each other. Besides, there are now laws to punish people who participate in cyber bullying.

Checklists & Reminders of what to do.

Phone calls:

You get a phone call from someone who you know, because the name and number are in your phone.

If you have time to talk, you answer the phone. Otherwise you can call back when you have time.

You get a call some someone who you don't know but you were expecting a call from this number at this time.

If it is the person that you were expecting.

Answer the call.

If the call is from someone else.

Hang up! Do not even listen to what he has to say. STRANGER DANGER!

You get a call from a number that is not in your phone and one that you do not recognize.

Later you can check your voicemail and listen to the message. If you think that it is important, ask someone that you trust if they too think that it is important. Look in the section in this book on SCAMS. The bad guys are tricky.

Messages:

- If you get a message from someone who you do not know.

    - It could be a weather or public service alert. Pay attention to it.

- If you get a message that contains a link (part of the message is underlined).

    - You should NOT click on that link unless you are sure who the message is from and that you were expecting a message like this from that person.

- If you get a message from several people who you know and someone is saying mean or nasty things about someone else, just do not respond unless you can defend the person being talked about.

    - Don't participate in cyber bullying. Be kind.

- You get a message from a friend.

    - Reply kindly.

Application/Game:

- You are playing a game and another player asks you questions about who you are, how old you are, where you live or other information that they do not need to play the game.

- DO NOT REPLY! If they are persistent. Stop playing that game.

• Only use Social Applications that have privacy modes. Use the privacy settings provided.

- Do NOT share personal data with strangers. STRANGER DANGER!

ACKNOWLEDGEMENTS

There are many people who helped to make this possible. I especially want to thank the following friends and family who took the time to review various drafts of this book, and provide feedback. To name a few they are: Tara, Virginia, Judy and Robert.

OTHER BOOKS BY THIS AUTHOR

The Continuing Adventures of Cyber Security Sam - Time Out is the first in the Cyber Security Sam TM series of books about a high school freshman who ends up working with the FBI to solve cyber-crime. This book is available at Book Baby, Amazon, or other places that similar adventure books are sold. The purpose of the Cyber Security Sam series is to influence young people to join the ranks of Cyber Sheep Dog and protect others. The next Cyber Security Sam book is being written now.

For more information about books and services by Rich Owen please go to the web page www.JohnnySecuritySeed.com.